GRAPHIC EXPEDITIONS

UNCOVERING MUMMIES

AN *Isabel Soto* ARCHAEOLOGY ADVENTURE

by Agnieszka Biskup

illustrated by Al Bigley, Cynthia Martin, and Bill Anderson

Consultant:
Ronald C. Schirmer
Associate Professor, Department of Anthropology
Minnesota State University, Mankato

Capstone

Mankato, Minnesota

Graphic Library is published by Capstone Press,
151 Good Counsel Drive, P.O. Box 669, Mankato, Minnesota 56002.
www.capstonepub.com

Printed in the United States of America in Stevens Point, Wisconsin.
052010
005774R

 Books published by Capstone Press are manufactured with paper
containing at least 10 percent post-consumer waste.

Library of Congress Cataloging-in-Publication Data
Biskup, Agnieszka.
  Uncovering mummies : an Isabel Soto archaeology adventure / by Agnieszka Biskup;
    illustrated by Al Bigley, Cynthia Martin, and Bill Anderson.
  p. cm. — (Graphic library. Graphic expeditions)
  Summary: "In graphic novel format, follows the adventures of Isabel Soto as she
researches mummies from around the world" — Provided by publisher.
  Includes bibliographical references and index.
  ISBN 978-1-4296-3412-0 (library binding)
  ISBN 978-1-4296-3900-2 (paperback)
  1. Mummies — Comic books, strips, etc. — Juvenile literature. 2. Graphic novels.
I. Bigley, Al, ill. II. Martin, Cynthia, 1961– ill. III. Anderson, Bill, 1963– ill. IV. Title. V. Series.
GN293.B576 2010
741.5973 — dc22   2009004955

Designer
Alison Thiele

Cover Artist
Tod G. Smith

Colorist
Krista Ward

Media Researcher
Wanda Winch

Editor
Aaron Sautter

Photo credits: Art Resource, N.Y./© The Trustees of The British Museum, 10;
Getty Images Inc./Time Life Pictures/Eliot Elisofon, 13

Design elements: Shutterstock/Chen Ping Hung (framed edge design); mmmm (world
map design); Mushakesa (abstract lines design); Najin (old parchment design)

TABLE OF CONTENTS

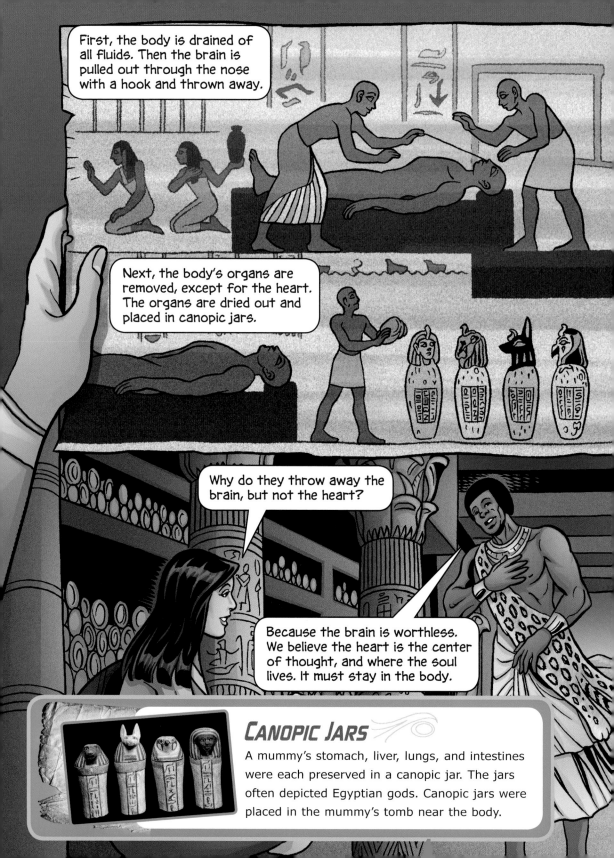

First, the body is drained of all fluids. Then the brain is pulled out through the nose with a hook and thrown away.

Next, the body's organs are removed, except for the heart. The organs are dried out and placed in canopic jars.

Why do they throw away the brain, but not the heart?

Because the brain is worthless. We believe the heart is the center of thought, and where the soul lives. It must stay in the body.

CANOPIC JARS

A mummy's stomach, liver, lungs, and intestines were each preserved in a canopic jar. The jars often depicted Egyptian gods. Canopic jars were placed in the mummy's tomb near the body.

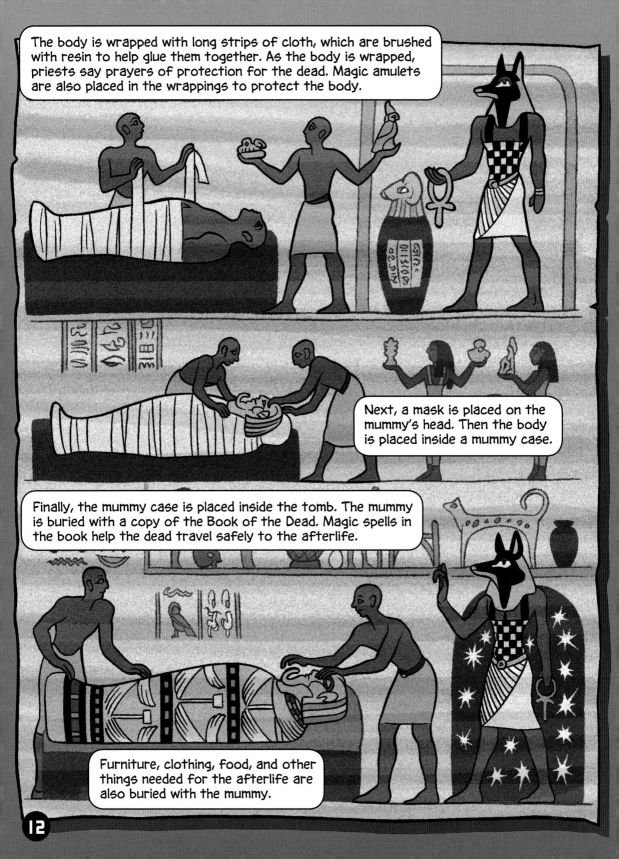

The body is wrapped with long strips of cloth, which are brushed with resin to help glue them together. As the body is wrapped, priests say prayers of protection for the dead. Magic amulets are also placed in the wrappings to protect the body.

Next, a mask is placed on the mummy's head. Then the body is placed inside a mummy case.

Finally, the mummy case is placed inside the tomb. The mummy is buried with a copy of the Book of the Dead. Magic spells in the book help the dead travel safely to the afterlife.

Furniture, clothing, food, and other things needed for the afterlife are also buried with the mummy.

THE SARCOPHAGUS

A mummy case was sometimes placed inside a heavy stone coffin called a sarcophagus. Only the wealthiest and most powerful people, such as pharaohs, were buried in a sarcophagus.

Have you ever heard of the Amulet of Fire?

There are many kinds of amulets. But I have never heard of the Amulet of Fire.

Perhaps you should talk to the amulet seller in the market.

Do you have an Amulet of Fire?

I've never heard of that amulet before. Can I interest you in a nice Eye of Horus instead? It has powerful protection against evil.

Drat. Maybe someone at the British Museum can tell me about the amulet.

X-rays can show us if the mummy was male or female, or if the person had health problems.

X-rays can even help us learn what kind of work the person did while alive.

Do most mummies have their arms crossed over their chests?

No, only pharaohs were buried with their arms in this position.

Let's see what we can find out about this mummy. I'll scan it with this advanced x-ray machine called a CT scanner.

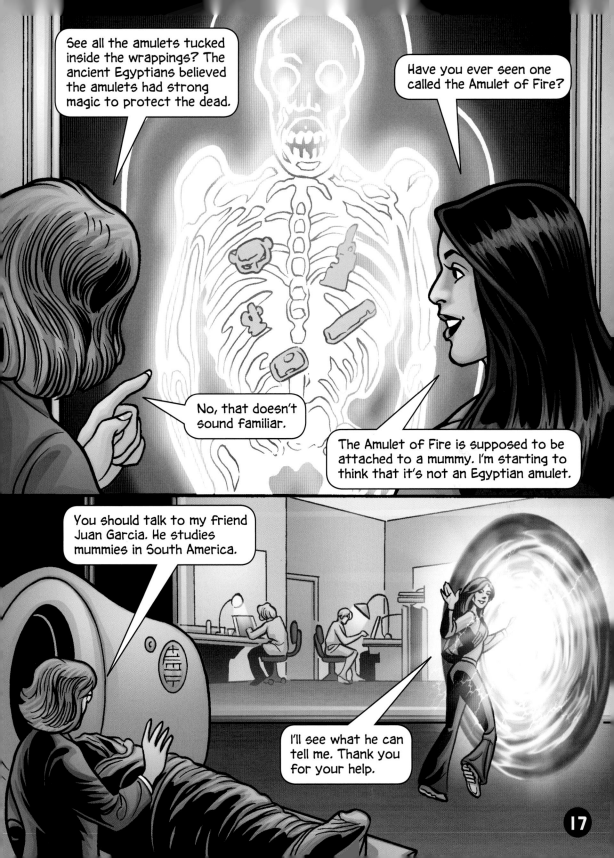

Andes Mountains, Peru, present day

Hi, Dr. Garcia. Could you tell me about South American mummies?

I'd be happy to. South America has some of the world's oldest mummies.

In Chile, the Chinchorro mummies date back at least 7,000 years.

They don't look like Egyptian mummies.

That's because the Chinchorro people made mummies differently. They removed the skin and organs first. Then they reinforced the bones with sticks. When the skin was dry, it was placed back on the bone and stick frame.

In Peru, bodies were preserved in "mummy bundles." The dead person's knees were drawn up to the chest. Then the body was wrapped in several layers of cloth. Over time, the body dried out to create a mummy.

Some mummies were made naturally. The Inca people offered human sacrifices to their gods high up in the mountains. The cold, dry climate froze the bodies and perfectly preserved them.

Have you ever seen a mummy wearing an Amulet of Fire?

No, but other natural mummies, like Otzi the Iceman or bog mummies, might hold some clues.

The Iceman was found in the Italian Alps. I'll go there first.

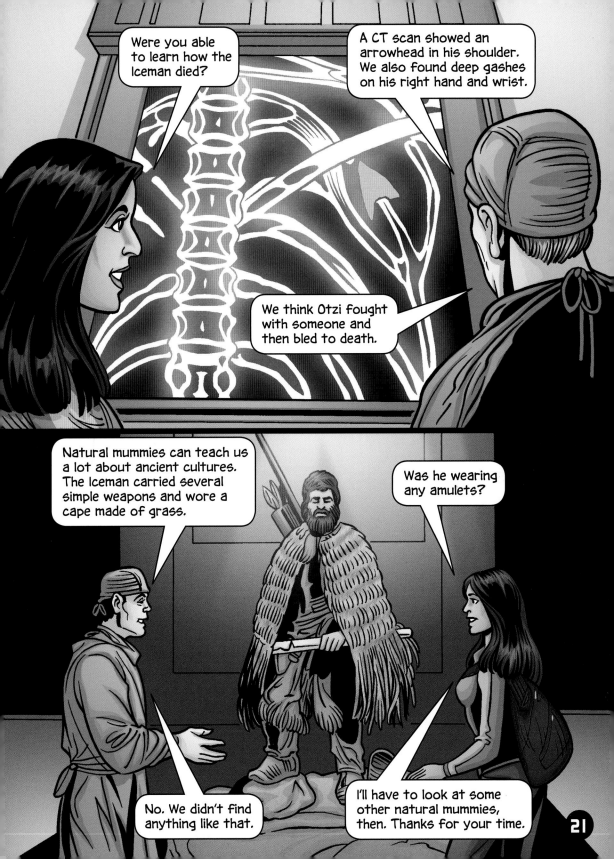

Excuse me, could you tell me about Tollund Man?

He's been dead for 2,400 years. A leather rope was tied around his neck. He may have been hanged.

We don't know if he was a criminal, or if he was a sacrifice to the gods.

Were any amulets found on his body?

No. Tollund Man just wore a leather cap and belt. His other clothes probably rotted away.

Hmm. I still haven't found anything about the amulet. And Dr. Powers is running out of time. I need to do more research.

BOG MUMMIES

Peat bogs are formed from decaying plants in marshy areas. Over time, the dense mass of rotting vegetation becomes peat, which can be burned for fuel. Over time, bog mummies turn a dark brown color as they lay in the peat. Chemicals in the peat tan and preserve the skin so it looks and feels like leather.

The mummified bodies of eight Inuit people were discovered in Greenland in 1972. They died around 1472. The cold, dry air had freeze-dried their bodies.

British sailor John Torrington was buried in the Canadian Arctic in 1846. Scientists dug up his body in 1984 to examine it. The freezing temperatures had perfectly preserved his body.

Several mummies were found in China's Takla Makan Desert in the 1980s. The bodies are thousands of years old. The dry conditions in the desert turned them into natural mummies.

I'm looking at all sorts of mummies. But I still can't find any mention of an Amulet of Fire.

When Russian leader Vladimir Lenin died in 1924, his body was embalmed and put on display. It can still be seen today in Moscow's Red Square.

There are thousands of mummies buried in tombs beneath the Capuchin Monastery in Palermo, Sicily. The oldest mummy dates back to 1599.

In New Guinea, people mummified bodies using smoke. Sometimes they hung bodies in trees to let the sun dry them out.

I don't think the amulet is real. It must be a myth. But I think I have an idea to save Dr. Powers.

MORE ABOUT MUMMIES

Mummification was an expensive process in ancient Egypt. If a person was wealthy, he or she could be made into a mummy and have an elaborate tomb. People who couldn't afford mummification were buried in pits.

Pharaohs aren't just buried in pyramids. About 3,600 years ago, the Egyptians began burying pharaohs in underground tombs in the Valley of the Kings. King Tut's tomb is located there. Archaeologists continue to explore the valley today.

The ancient Egyptians also mummified cats, bulls, birds, and even crocodiles. Many Egyptian gods were linked to certain animals. The sacred animals were mummified and buried as gifts to the gods.

Ancient mummies have not always been treated with respect. In the Middle Ages, Egyptian mummies were ground up into "mummy powder" and used as medicine. Mummies were sometimes used as fuel for fires too. Until the early 1900s, Egyptian mummies were often ground into a fine brown powder to make an artist's paint called "mummy brown."

Many Chinchorro mummies had delicate clay masks placed on their faces. Several also wore wigs or clay helmets.

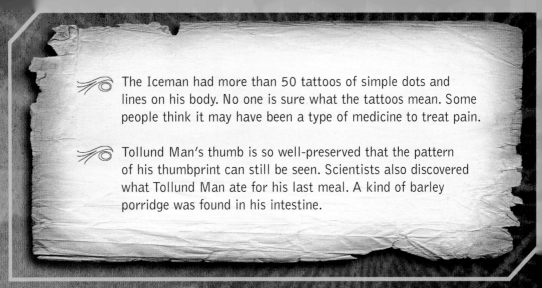

The Iceman had more than 50 tattoos of simple dots and lines on his body. No one is sure what the tattoos mean. Some people think it may have been a type of medicine to treat pain.

Tollund Man's thumb is so well-preserved that the pattern of his thumbprint can still be seen. Scientists also discovered what Tollund Man ate for his last meal. A kind of barley porridge was found in his intestine.

MORE ABOUT

NAME: Dr. Isabel "Izzy" Soto
DEGREES: History and Anthropology
BUILD: Athletic **HAIR:** Dark Brown
EYES: Brown **HEIGHT:** 5' 7"

W.I.S.P.: The Worldwide Inter-dimensional Space/Time Portal developed by Max Axiom at Axiom Laboratory.

BACKSTORY: Dr. Isabel "Izzy" Soto caught the history bug as a little girl. Every night, her grandfather told her about his adventures exploring ancient ruins in South America. He believed lost cultures teach people a great deal about history.

Izzy's love of cultures followed her to college. She studied history and anthropology. On a research trip to Thailand, she discovered an ancient stone with mysterious energy. Izzy took the stone to Super Scientist Max Axiom, who determined that the stone's energy cuts across space and time. Harnessing the power of the stone, he built a device called the W.I.S.P. It opens windows to any place and any time. Izzy now travels through time to see history unfold before her eyes. Although she must not change history, she can observe and investigate historical events.

amulet (AM-yoo-let) — a small charm believed to protect the wearer from harm

canopic jar (kuh-NO-pik JAR) — a jar in which the ancient Egyptians preserved the organs of a dead person

CT scanner (SEE TEE SKAN-ur) — a special x-ray machine that takes hundreds of pictures to create a 3-D image of a person's body; CT scans can show soft tissues like internal organs.

embalm (im-BALM) — to preserve a dead body so it does not decay

kidnap (KID-nap) — to capture a person and keep him or her as a prisoner, usually until demands are met

natron (NAY-tron) — a type of salt used by ancient Egyptians to create mummies

organ (OR-guhn) — a part of the body that does a certain job

peat (PEET) — partly decayed plant matter found in bogs and swamps

pharaoh (FAIR-oh) — a king of ancient Egypt

ransom (RAN-suhm) — money or objects that are demanded before someone who is being held captive can be set free

resin (REZ-in) — a sticky substance that comes from the sap of some trees

sarcophagus (sar-KAH-fuh-guhs) — a stone coffin; the ancient Egyptians sometimes placed an inner coffin into a sarcophagus.

temple (TEM-puhl) — a building used for worship

tomb (TOOM) — a grave, room, or building that holds a dead body

x-ray (EKS-ray) — a photograph of the inside of a person's body

READ MORE

Bolton, Anne. *Pyramids and Mummies.* New York: Simon and Schuster, 2008.

Burgan, Michael. *The Curse of King Tut's Tomb.* Graphic History. Mankato, Minn.: Capstone Press, 2005.

Halls, Kelly Milner. *Mysteries of the Mummy Kids.* Plain City, Ohio: Darby Creek Publishing, 2007.

Martin, Michael. *Inca Mummies: Sacrifices and Rituals.* Mummies. Mankato, Minn.: Capstone Press, 2005.

Putnam, James. *Mummy.* Eyewitness Books. New York: DK Publishing, 2009.

INTERNET SITES

FactHound offers a safe, fun way to find Internet sites related to this book. All of the sites on FactHound have been researched by our staff.

Here's all you do:

Visit *www.facthound.com*

FactHound will fetch the best sites for you!

INDEX